A Daybook for Writers

Transforming Writers into Authors

written by

Manifest Publishing

A Daybook for Writers/ CaZ -- 1st ed.
ISBN-10:1-944913-15-7
ISBN-13:978-1-944913-15-1

DEDICATION

Tonja Waring, Gary Barnes, and Jessica Peterson
Thank you. It is with your guidance that I have truly grown into my role as the Writer Success Coach.

Turn beliefs into action to achieve dreams!

CONTENTS

"By now, it is probably very late at night, and you have stayed up to read this book when you should have gone to sleep. If this is the case, then I commend you for falling into my trap. It is a writer's greatest pleasure to hear that someone was kept up until the unholy hours of the morning reading one of his books. It goes back to authors being terrible people who delight in the suffering of others. Plus, we get a kickback from the caffeine industry..."

~Brandon Sanderson

LET US BEGIN...

Why a Daybook?

My profession is writer. I am an author. And a teacher.

I have worn many job-hats in my life. Lifeguard. Waitress. Insurance Clerk. Medical librarian. Technical writer. Fiction writer. Computer Instructor. Publishing Sales Rep. Marketing Consultant. Ghostwriter, Technical Virtual Assistant. Computer Training Center owner. Publisher, Editor, Writer Success Coach. There are so many more. This might seem a long list, yet for any artist who has searched for a way to earn a living while pursuing her art, you will know this is a short list.

In every career or business iteration I have pursued, the constant always centered around writing and teaching, usually in combination.

Why a daybook? There is a conceptual difference between a diary or journal and a daybook. In a diary, for instance, one typically records experiences. In a daybook, one records a response; a moment in time for that day. It's a marvelous tool for a writer (or any creative person) to use as a springboard to being creative.

Why a daybook? I went looking for a daybook for myself—I would have bought another author's creation happily. I found many. Most were targeted to specific types of creative or emotive pursuits. Not one book that I found, however, focused on writers.

This book is focused on writers. It is comprised of 12 sections that loosely conform to months. Within each section are 31 quotes from writers. I chose quotes from writers talking about the process, the pain, the joy of being a writer. Each quote is followed by lightly-lined space. Room for you reflect or begin your own conversation around the quote's topic.

Why a daybook? Quite simply, I am a writer and a teacher and a daybook blends my two passions perfectly.

Why a daybook? This is literally the book I woke up with fully written in my head. I posted on Facebook that I was going to write a book that day—not start, write the first draft entirely. And I did. This book.

It is a creativity tool that my muse guided me to create. I will use it. And I hope you will, too.

CHAPTER TWO

Suggestions for Using This Book

First, have fun with this. Fit reading this book into your daily schedule. More importantly, take five minutes (or more) to write in response to what you read.

Does that mean you must stick to the topic of the quote for the day? Absolutely. And Absolutely not!

The goal is for you to develop the habit of writing daily. Simply write as much or as little as fits into your life each day. And write about whatever piques your interest at the time.

Do you have to write first thing in the morning? Only if that's the time you choose. This is a small book easily transported. Take it with you.

Do you have five minutes in your day somewhere? Everyone does (even if it's in the bathroom!). Perhaps you'll put this book in your car's glovebox and pull it out when you are waiting to pick up the kids from soccer practice. Or maybe you could use a five-minute creativity break at work—pull out your daybook!

Find those few minutes every day. The key is to use this book as best fits your world. Use it as a tool to jumpstart your creative engine and keep it humming in good working order.

Note that there are no dates printed for you. Each section begins with a list of the months. Circle the current month and insert the date under the quote as you write.

Use these quotes and the time you devote to this book as a daily prompt. Use it as an occasional prompt. Ignore the date prompt altogether. Write your response in the book or on your preferred digital device. The book is flexible. Your life is flexible.

The choice for how and when you use this book is yours. The key is to make that choice and do it every day.

Happy Writing!

"I write to find strength.

I write to become the person that hides inside me.

I write to light the way through the darkness for others.

I write to be seen and heard.

I write to be near those I love.

I write by accident, promptings, purposefully and anywhere there is paper.

I write because my heart speaks a different language that someone needs to hear.

I write past the embarrassment of exposure.

I write because hypocrisy doesn't need answers, rather it needs questions to heal.

I write myself out of nightmares.

I write because I am nostalgic, romantic and demand happy endings.

I write to remember.

I write knowing conversations don't always take place.

I write because speaking can't be reread.

I write to sooth a mind that races.

I write because you can play on the page like a child left alone in the sand.

I write because my emotions belong to the moon; high tide, low tide.

I write knowing I will fall on my words, but no one will say it was for very long.

I write because I want to paint the world the way I see love should be.

I write to provide a legacy.

I write to make sense out of senselessness.

I write knowing I will be killed by my own words, stabbed by critics, crucified by both misunderstanding and understanding.

I write for the haters, the lovers, the lonely, the brokenhearted and the dreamers.

I write because one day someone will tell me my emotions were not a waste of time.

I write because God loves stories.

I write because one day I will be gone, but what I believed and felt will live on."

— Shannon L. Alder

MONTH ONE

January
February
March
April
May
June

July
August
September
October
November
December

"Writers write. It's what we do. One word, one letter, one concept, one scene, one character, one bite of story at a time. We write. And then? We write some more."

~ CaZ

(date)

"Focus is driven by vision and planning. The actions we take and the progress we make continually reinforces our focus and allows us to remain on track."

~ CaZ

(date)

"My writing is an overflow of the wine glass of my life, not a basin in which I wash out my ideals and expectations."

~ C. JoyBell

(date)

"It's the witching hour once more- When the Muse comes out to play. He calls me through that magic door- Where galaxies of worlds await!"

~ Belle Whittington

(date)

"I have told people that writing this book has been like brushing away dirt from a fossil. What a load of shit. It has been like hacking away at a freezer with a screwdriver."

~ Amy Pohler

(date)

"Doors open when passion + purpose are ignited + shared. Write what you love."

~ CaZ

(date)

"Self pity is easily the most destructive of the non-pharmaceutical narcotics; it is addictive, gives momentary pleasure and separates the victim from reality."

~ John Gardner

(date)

"Successful writing is not about publishing or money. A writer is one who writes and a successful writer is one who writes consistently and persistently."

~ CaZ

(date)

"If you can write each day, do it, and meet a quota. Minimum 350 words a day. A baboon can do 350 words a day. Don't be shown up by a baboon."

~ James Scott Bell

(date)

"No tears in the writer, no tears in the reader. No surprise in the writer, no surprise in the reader."

~ Robert Frost

"Don't market yourself. Editors and readers don't know what they want until they see it. Scratch what itches. Write what you need to write, feed the hunger for meaning in your life. Play at the serious questions of life and death."

~ Donald M. Murray

(date) ________

"It's your story and nobody can tell it better.

~ CaZ

(date) ________

"You have to write the book that wants to be written. And if the book will be too difficult for grown-ups, then you write it for children."

~ Madeleine L'Engle

(date)

"You write to communicate to the hearts and minds of others what's burning inside you. And you edit to let the fire show through the smoke."

~ Arthur Plotnik

(date)

"The bridge between the words glamour and grammar is magic. According to the OED, glamour evolved through an ancient association between learning and enchantment."

~ Roy Peter Clark

(date)

"Make a difference. Leave a legacy."

~ Victoria A. Hudson

(date)

"A book, too, can be a star, a living fire to lighten the darkness, leading out into the expanding universe."

~ Madeleine L'Engle

(date)

"Words to me were magic. You could say a word and it could conjure up all kinds of images or feelings or a chilly sensation or whatever."

~ Amy Tan

(date)

"I didn't find my story; it found me, as autobiography always does: finds you out in your deepest most private places."

~ Kelly Cherry

(date)

"Stories make us more alive, more human, more courageous, more loving."

~ Madeleine L'Engle

(date)

"Write what disturbs you, what you fear, what you have not been willing to speak about. Be willing to be split open."

~ Natalie Goldberg

(date)

"The role of a writer is not to say what we can all say, but what we are unable to say."

~ Anais Nin

(date)

"Being a writer is a very peculiar sort of a job: it's always you versus a blank sheet of paper (or a blank screen) and quite often the blank piece of paper wins."

~ Neil Gaiman

(date)

"I can't write without a reader. It's precisely like a kiss—you can't do it alone."

~ John Cheever

"I'm asked if I think the university stifles writers. My opinion is that they don't stifle enough of them. There's many a best-seller that could have been prevented by a good teacher."

~ Flannery O'Connor

(date)

"So what? All writers are lunatics!"

~ Cornelia Funke

(date)

"So the writer who breeds more words than he needs, is making a chore for the reader who reads."

~ Dr. Seuss

(date)

"A little talent is a good thing to have if you want to be a writer. But the only real requirement is the ability to remember every scar."

~ Stephen King

(date)

"Writing [is] like singing on a boat during a terrible storm at sea. You can't stop the raging storm, but singing can change the hearts and spirits of the people who are together on that ship."

~ Anne Lamott

(date)

"As a writer, you should not judge, you should understand."

~ Ernest Hemingway

(date)

"It's the process of writing and life that matters. Too many writers have written great books and gone insane or alcoholic or killed themselves. This process teaches about sanity. We are trying to become sane along with our poems and stories."

~ Natalie Goldberg

THOUGHTS AND NOTES

(date)

January	July
February	August
March	September
April	October
May	November
June	December

"Who is more to be pitied, a writer bound and gagged by policemen or one living in perfect freedom who has nothing more to say?"

~ Kurt Vonnegut Jr.

(date)

"A person is a fool to become a writer. His only compensation is absolute freedom. He has no master except his own soul, and that, I am sure, is why he does it."

~ Roald Dahl

(date)

"Most basic material a writer works with is acquired before the age of fifteen."

~ Willa Cather

(date)

"Publish your book and you are instantly seen as an achiever, a person who can accomplish most any task. The perception is that as the author of a published book, you have great discipline and fortitude."

~ CaZ

(date)

"Deliver me from writers who say the way they live doesn't matter. I'm not sure a bad person can write a good book. If art doesn't make us better, then what on earth is it for."

~ Alice Walker

(date)

"Even the most productive writers are expert dwadlers."

~ Donald M. Murray

(date)

"What people value in their books—and thus what they count as literature—really tells you more about them than it does about the book."

~ Brent Weeks

(date)

"I think that writers are made, not born or created out of dreams of childhood trauma—that becoming a writer (or a painter, actor, director, dancer, and so on) is a direct result of conscious will."

~ Stephen King

(date)

"Writing is one of those things where you just have to do it. There will be far more people to discourage you than to encourage you. The time never comes to you, the inspiration doesn't come to you. You just sit down and do it."

~ James Lee Burke

(date)

"You keep writing because it's the only way to finish the book."

~ James Scott Bell

(date)

"We must become writers who accept things as they are, come to love the details, and step forward with a yes on our lips so there can be no more noes in the world, noes that invalidate life and stop these details from continuing."

~ Natalie Goldberg

(date)

"Some things have to be believed to be seen."

~ Madeleine L'Engle

(date)

"A book will speak for you in a way that a 30-second elevator speech cannot. Authoring a book is easily one of the best investments you will make for your business and will catapult you to leading authority."

~ CaZ

(date)

"Description begins in the writer's imagination, but should finish in the reader's."

~ Stephen King

(date)

"A writer is a person who cares what words mean, what they say, how they say it. Writers know words are their way towards truth and freedom, and so they use them with care, with thought, with fear, with delight."

~ Ursula K. Le Guin

(date)

"Stop aspiring and start writing. If you're writing, you're a writer."

~ Alan W. Watts

(date)

"If you want to be a writer-stop talking about it and sit down and write!"

~ Jackie Collins

(date)

"Writing a book is like doing a huge jigsaw puzzle, unendurably slow at first, almost self-propelled at the end."

~ James Richardson

(date)

"This is what separates artists from ordinary people: the belief, deep in our hearts, that if we build our [sand] castles well enough, somehow the ocean won't wash them away. I think this is a wonderful kind of person to be."

~ Anne Lamont

(date)

"Don't be 'a writer'. Be writing."

~ William Faulkner

(date)

"He asked, "What makes a man a writer?" "Well," I said, "it's simple. You either get it down on paper, or jump off a bridge."

~ Charles Burkowski

(date)

"Writer's block is a fancy term made up by whiners so they can have an excuse to drink alcohol."

~ Steve Martin

(date)

"Which of us has not felt that the character we are reading in the printed page is more real than the person standing beside us?"

~ Cornelia Funke

(date)

"If grammar is the skeleton of expression and usage the flesh and blood, then style is the personality."

~ Arthur Plotnik,

(date)

"I didn't find my story; it found me, as autobiography always does: finds you out in your deepest most private places."

~ Kelly Cherry,

(date)

"Books are uniquely portable magic."

~ Stephen King

(date)

"Write what disturbs you, what you fear, what you have not been willing to speak about. Be willing to be split open."

~ Natalie Goldberg

(date)

"People who read want one of two things: knowledge or entertainment. When you can give them both, so much the better."

~ James Scott Bell

(date)

"When you devote time to understanding your gifts and talents, you develop a stronger sense of who you are, what you can contribute, and how you can use your life experience to nourish your writing."

~ CaZ

(date)

"Write like you're in love. Edit like you're in charge."

~ James Scott Bell

(date)

"The longer I am a writer--so long now that my writing finger is periodically numb--the better I understand what writing is; what its function is; what it is supposed to do. I learn that the writer's pen is a microphone held up to the mouths of ancestors and even stones of long ago. That once given permission by the writer--a fool, and so why should one fear? - horses, dogs, rivers, and, yes, chickens can step forward and expound on their lives. The magic of this is not so much in the power of the microphone as in the ability of the nonhuman object or animal to BE and the human animal to PERCEIVE ITS BEING."

~ Alice Walker

THOUGHTS AND NOTES

(date)

(date)

January	July
February	August
March	September
April	October
May	November
June	December

"Read a thousand books, and your words will flow like a river."

~ Lisa See

(date)

"Put down everything that comes into your head and then you're a writer. But an author is one who can judge his own stuff's worth, without pity, and destroy most of it."

~ Colette

(date)

"Following your dreams—that is freedom. Even when it's hard or scary and you feel like giving up—even then, there's something about following your heart's passion that feels right and purposeful. If your dream is to write, then writing is right."

~ CaZ

(date)

"If a writer falls in love with you, you can never die."

~ Mik Everett

(date)

"If you have any young friends who aspire to become writers, the second greatest favor you can do them is to present them with copies of The Elements of Style. The first greatest, of course, is to shoot them now, while they're happy."

~ Dorothy Parker

(date)

"A professional writer is an amateur who didn't quit."

~ Richard Bach

(date)

"If you want to be a writer, you must do two things above all others: read a lot and write a lot. There's no way around these two things that I'm aware of, no shortcut."

~ Stephen King

(date)

"Give yourself permission to be bad. Write first, polish later."

~ James Scott Bell,

(date)

"By using words well they strengthen their souls. Story-tellers and poets spend their lives learning that skill and art of using words well. And their words make the souls of their readers stronger, brighter, deeper."

~ Ursula K. Le Guin

(date)

"Some editors are failed writers, but so are most writers."

~ T.S. Eliot

(date)

"Two hours of writing fiction leaves this writer completely drained. For those two hours he has been in a different place with totally different people."

~ Roald Dahl

(date)

"I love being a writer. What I can't stand is the paperwork."

~ Peter De Vries

(date)

"Whenever I'm asked why Southern writers particularly have a penchant for writing about freaks, I say it is because we are still able to recognize one."

~ Flannery O'Connor

(date)

"Writing is like driving at night in the fog. You can only see as far as your headlights, but you can make the whole trip that way."

~ E.L. Doctorow

"At night, when the objective world has slunk back into its cavern and left dreamers to their own, there come inspirations and capabilities impossible at any less magical and quiet hour. No one knows whether or not he is a writer unless he has tried writing at night."

~ H.P. Lovecraft.

(date)

"Writers are the exorcists of their own demons."

~ Mario Vargas Llosa

(date)

"Nothing's a better cure for writer's block than to eat ice cream right out of the carton."

~ Don Roff

(date)

"There's an epigram tacked to my office bulletin board, pinched from a magazine - Wanting to meet an author because you like his work is like wanting to meet a duck because you like pâté."

~ Margaret Atwood

(date)

"Some writers enjoy writing, I am told. Not me. I enjoy having written."

~ George R.R. Martin

(date)

"Keep writing, keep faith in the idea that you have unique stories to tell, and tell them. I meet far too many people who are going to be writers 'someday.'"

~ Robin Hobb

(date)

"Don't listen to people who tell you that very few people get published and you won't be one of them. Don't listen to your friend who says you are better that Tolkien and don't have to try any more."

~ Robin Hobb

(date)

"The second thing you have to do to be a writer is to keep on writing."

~ Robin Hobb

(date)

"Any writer worth his salt writes to please himself... It's a self-exploratory operation that is endless. An exorcism of not necessarily his demon, but of his divine discontent."

~ Harper Lee

(date)

"Indeed, I would venture to guess that Anon, who wrote so many poems without signing them, was often a woman."

~ Virginia Woolf"

"When I got older I decided I wanted to be a real writer. I tried to write about real things. I wanted to describe the world, because to live in an undescribed world was too lonely."

~ Nicole Krauss

(date)

"You can't blame a writer for what the characters say."

~ Truman Capote

(date)

"I don't think all writers are sad, she said. I think it's the other way around- all sad people write."

~ Lang Leav

(date) ________

"In order to write the book you want to write, in the end you have to become the person you need to become to write that book."

~ Junot Díaz

(date) ________

"Tell the truth as you understand it. If you're a writer you have a moral obligation to do this. And it is a revolutionary act—truth is always subversive."

~ Anne Lamott

(date)

"Write straight into the emotional center of things."

~ Anne Lamott

(date)

"...a writer has the duty to be good, not lousy; true, not false; lively, not dull; accurate, not full of error. He should tend to lift people up, not lower them down. Writers do not merely reflect and interpret life, they inform and shape life."

~ E.B. White

THOUGHTS AND NOTES

(date)

(date)

January	July
February	August
March	September
April	October
May	November
June	December

"I have advice for people who want to write. There are three things that are important: First, if you want to write, you need to keep an honest, unpublishable journal that nobody reads, nobody but you."

~ Madeleine L'Engle

(date)

"And second, you need to read. You can't be a writer if you're not a reader. It's the great writers who teach us how to write."

~ Madeleine L'Engle

(date)

"The third thing is to write. Just write a little bit every day. Even if it's for only half an hour – write, write, write."

~ Madeleine L'Engle"

(date)

"I have no taste for either poverty or honest labor, so writing is the only recourse left for me."

~ Hunter S. Thompson

(date)

"Author-ity. I love the clarity of this word. It combines two vital concepts and brings their correlation immediately into view. You are an author when you, as an authority, have published your expertise."

~ CaZ

(date)

"Don't classify me, read me. I'm a writer, not a genre."

~ Carlos Fuentes

(date)

"No black woman writer in this culture can write "too much". Indeed, no woman writer can write "too much"...No woman has ever written enough."

~ bell hooks

(date)

"When male authors write love stories, the heroine tends to end up dead."

~ Susan Elizabeth Phillips

(date)

"Writing is something that you don't know how to do. You sit down and it's something that happens, or it may not happen. So, how can you teach anybody how to write?"

~ Charles Bukowski

"I am a strong believer in the tyranny, the dictatorship, the absolute authority of the writer."

~ Philip Pullman

"Write while the heat is in you. The writer who postpones the recording of his thoughts uses an iron which has cooled to burn a hole with. He cannot inflame the minds of his audience."

~ Henry David Thoreau

(date)

"I must be lean + write + make worlds beside this to live in."

~ Sylvia Plath

(date)

"Making love to me is amazing. Wait, I meant: making love, to me, is amazing. The absence of two little commas nearly transformed me into a sex god."

~ Dark Jar Tin Zoo

(date)

"Your intuition knows what to write, so get out of the way."

~ Ray Bradbury

(date)

"I'd like to have money. And I'd like to be a good writer. These two can come together, and I hope they will, but if that's too adorable, I'd rather have money."

~ Dorothy Parker

(date)

"A writer must teach himself that the basest of all things is to be afraid."

~ William Faulkner

(date)

"If a writer stops observing he is finished. Experience is communicated by small details intimately observed."

~ Ernest Hemingway

(date)

"It is impossible to discourage the real writers - they don't give a damn what you say, they're going to write."

~ Sinclair Lewis

(date)

"Be ruthless about protecting writing days...guard the time allotted to writing as a Hungarian Horntail guards its firstborn egg."

~ J.K. Rowling

(date)

"My most important piece of advice to all you would-be writers: When you write, try to leave out all the parts readers skip."

~ Elmore Leonard

(date)

"The semi-colon is a burp, a hiccup. It's a drunk staggering out of the saloon at 2 a.m., grabbing your lapels on the way and asking you to listen to one more story."

~ James Scott Bell

(date) ________

"You write to communicate to the hearts and minds of others what's burning inside you. And you edit to let the fire show through the smoke."

~ Arthur Plotnik

(date) ________

"You get into the habit of writing every day so that when she shows up, you have the maximum chance of catching her, bashing her on the head, and squeezing every last drop out of that bitch."

~ Lili St. Crow

(date)

"A writer is a writer because even when there is no hope, even when nothing you do shows any sign of promise, you keep writing anyway."

~ Junot Díaz

(date)

"Every morning I jump out of bed and step on a landmine. The landmine is me. After the explosion, I spend the rest of the day putting the pieces together."

~ Ray Bradbury

(date)

"A writer should write what he has to say and not speak it."

~ Ernest Hemingway

(date)

"You know how writers are... they create themselves as they create their work. Or perhaps they create their work in order to create themselves."

~ Orson Scott Card

(date)

"Dance above the surface of the world. Let your thoughts lift you into creativity that is not hampered by opinion."

~ Red Haircrow

(date)

"Writing is a lonely job. Having someone who believes in you makes a lot of difference. They don't have to makes speeches. Just believing is usually enough."

~ Stephen King

(date)

"A writer, I think, is someone who pays attention to the world."

~ Susan Sontag

(date)

"I've had to keep defining and defending myself as a writer every single day of my adult life -- constantly reminding and re-reminding my soul and the cosmos that I'm very serious about the business of creative living, and that I will never stop creating, no matter what the outcome, and no matter how deep my anxieties and insecurities may be."

~ Elizabeth Gilbert

THOUGHTS AND NOTES

(date)

(date)

January
February
March
April
May
June
July
August
September
October
November
December

"We are not nouns, we are verbs. I am not a thing... I am a person who does things - I write, I act. I never know what I'm going to do next. I think you can be imprisoned if you think of yourself as a noun."

~ Stephen Fry

(date)

"A great writer reveals the truth even when he or she does not wish to."

~ Tom Bissell

(date)

"Because this business of becoming conscious, of being a writer, is ultimately about asking yourself, How alive am I willing to be?"

~ Anne Lamott

(date)

"People often ask me why my style is so simple. It is, in fact, deceptively simple, for no two sentences are alike. It is clarity that I am striving to attain, not simplicity."

~ Ruskin Bond

(date)

"Writing a book is a long, exhausting struggle, like a long bout of painful illness. One would never undertake such a thing if one were not driven by some demon whom one can neither resist nor understand."

~ George Orwell

(date)

"Every writer I know has trouble writing."

~ Joseph Heller

(date)

"I want to be clear about this. If you wrote from experience, you'd get maybe one book, maybe three poems. Writers write from empathy."

~ Nikki Giovanni

(date)

"Realism can break a writer's heart."

~ Salman Rushdie

(date)

"A young writer is easily tempted by the allusive and ethereal and ironic and reflective, but the declarative is at the bottom of most good writing."

~ Garrison Keillor

(date)

"The whole world's writing novels, but nobody's reading them."

~ Robert Galbraith

(date)

"Write. Write more. Write even more. Write even more than that. Write when you don't want to. Write when you do. Write when you have something to say. Write when you don't. Write every day. Keep writing."

~ Brian Clark

(date)

"The thing all writers do best is find ways to avoid writing."

~ Alan Dean Foster

(date)

"Really, becoming a writer sounds more like a mental illness than a professional choice."

~ Shannon Hale

(date)

"When it's in a book I don't think it'll hurt any more ...exist any more. One of the things writing does is wipe things out. Replace them."

~ Marguerite Duras

(date)

"Borges said there are four stories to tell: a love story between two people, a love story between three people, the struggle for power and the voyage. All of us writers rewrite these same stories ad infinitum."

~ Paulo Coelho

(date)

"You must stay drunk on writing so reality cannot destroy you."

~ Ray Bradbury

(date)

"The job of the writer is to take a close and uncomfortable look at the world they inhabit, the world we all inhabit, and the job of the novel is to make the corpse stink."

~ Walter Mosley

(date)

"We are great writers on the same dreadful typewriter"

~ Allen Ginsberg

(date)

"I'm not a writer with a drinking problem, I'm a drinker with a writing problem."

~ Dorothy Parker

(date)

"I am a writer of books in retrospect. I talk in order to understand; I teach in order to learn."

~ Robert Frost

(date)

"Once the writer in every individual comes to life (and that time is not far off), we are in for an age of universal deafness and lack of understanding."

~ Milan Kundera

(date)

"Writers will happen in the best of families."

~ Rita Mae Brown

(date)

"Almost everyone can remember losing his or her virginity, and most writers can remember the first book he/she put down thinking: I can do better than this. Hell, I am doing better than this!"

~ Stephen King

(date)

"There is no such thing as an aspiring writer. You are a writer. Period."

~ Matthew Reilly

(date)

"Women writers make for rewarding (and efficient) lovers. They are clever liars to fathers and husbands; yet they never hold their tongues too long, nor keep ardent typing fingers still."

~ Roman Payne

(date)

"A writer is someone who has taught his mind to misbehave."

~ Oscar Wilde

(date)

"When I begin to doubt my ability to work the word, I simply read another writer and know I have nothing to worry about. My contest is only with myself...."

~ Charles Bukowski

(date)

Good writers are good readers."

~ James Scott Bell

(date)

"Start telling the stories that only you can tell, because there'll always be better writers than you and there'll always be smarter writers than you. ...but you are the only you."

~ Neil Gaiman

(date)

"Writers are really people who write books...because they are dissatisfied with the books which they could buy but do not like."

~ Walter Benjamin

"My job as a writer is simple. Write a book I'm proud of, and present it as a gift to the world.
Some will love it.
Some will hate it.
That's the nature of art."

~ Kathleen Baldwin

THOUGHTS AND NOTES

(date)

January
February
March
April
May
June
July
August
September
October
November
December

"I want to write about people I love, and put them into a fictional world spun out of my own mind, not the world we actually have, because the world we actually have does not meet my standards."

~ Philip K. Dick

(date)

"Being a writer brings out a sassy woman inside me, and I love her so."

~ Anna Bayes

(date)

"Writing is a concentrated form of thinking...a young writer sees that with words he can place himself more clearly into the world."

~ Don DeLillo

(date)

"There's no such thing as writer's block. That was invented by people in California who couldn't write."

~ Terry Pratchett

(date)

"The prime function of the children's book writer is to write a book that is so absorbing, exciting, funny, fast and beautiful that the child will fall in love with it."

~ Roald Dahl

(date)

"Writers write while dreamers procrastinate."

~ Besa Kosova

(date)

"Writing, real writing, should leave a small sweet bruise somewhere on the writer... and on the reader."

~ Clarissa Pinkola Estés

(date)

"You sit down... at approximately the same time every day. This is how you train your unconscious to kick in for you creatively."

~ Anne Lamott

(date)

"You wrote down that you were a writer by profession. It sounded to me like the loveliest euphemism I had ever heard. When was writing ever your profession? It's never been anything but your religion."

~ J.D. Salinger

(date)

"Are you a real writer? Then keep writing. And don't stop. Ever."

~ James Scott Bell

(date)

"Life cannot defeat a writer who is in love with writing - for life itself is a writer's love until death."

~ Edna Ferber

(date)

"The writer must be universal in sympathy and an outcast by nature: only then can he see clearly."

~ Julian Barnes

(date)

"To write a story, to read a story, is to be a refugee from the state of refugees. Writers and readers seek a solution to the problem..."

~ Mohsin Hamid

(date)

"A word is not the same with one writer as it is with another. One tears it from his guts. The other pulls it out of his overcoat pocket."

~ Charles Péguy

(date)

"Whenever I'm asked what advice I have for young writers, I always say that the first thing is to read, and to read a lot. The second thing is to write. And the third thing, which I think is absolutely vital, is to tell stories and listen closely to the stories you're being told."

~ John Green

(date) ________

"Ink, a Drug."

~ Vladimir Nabokov

(date) ________

"You learn to write by writing, and by reading and thinking about how writers have created their characters and invented their stories. If you are not a reader, don't even think about being a writer."

~ Jean M. Auel

(date)

"If you can quit, then quit. If you can't quit, you're a writer."

~ R.A. Salvatore

(date)

"If you are not afraid of the voices inside you, you will not fear the critics outside you."

~ Natalie Goldberg

(date)

"Are you a born writer? In the end the question can only be answered by action. Do it or don't do it."

~ Steven Pressfield

(date)

"That's why writers write—to say things loudly with ink. To give feet to thoughts; to make quiet, still feelings loudly heard."

~ Tarryn Fisher

(date)

"Writing is magic, as much the water of life as any other creative art. The water is free. So drink. Drink and be filled up."

~ Stephen King

(date)

"You Must Write. Finish What Your Start. You Must Refrain from Rewriting, Except to Editorial Order. You Must Put Your Story on the Market. You Must Keep it on the Market until it has Sold"

~ Robert A. Heinlein

(date)

"I can shake off everything if I write; my sorrows disappear; my courage is reborn."

~ Anne Frank

(date)

"Every story has already been told. There is really no reason to ever write another novel. Except that each writer brings to the table something that no one else in the history of time has ever had."

~ Anna Quindlen

(date)

"Long before I wrote stories, I listened for stories."

~ Eudora Welty

(date)

"If you want to be a writer, you have to write every day... You don't go to a well once but daily. You don't skip a child's breakfast or forget to wake up in the morning..."

~ Walter Mosley

(date)

"Don't tell me the moon is shining, show me the glint of light on broken glass."

~ Bernard Cornwell

(date)

"The library, on the other hand, has no biases. The information is all there for you to interpret. You don't have someone telling you what to think. You discover it for yourself."

~ Ray Bradbury

(date)

"Writing about a writer's block is better than not writing at all"

~ Charles Bukowski

(date)

"Writers are magicians. They write down words, and, if they're good, you believe that what they write is real, just as you believe a good magician has pulled the coins out of your ear, or made his assistant disappear. But the words on the page have no connection to the person who wrote them. Writers live other peoples' lives for them."

~ W.P. Kinsella

THOUGHTS AND NOTES

(date)

January	July
February	August
March	September
April	October
May	November
June	December

"You can you read a hundred books on wisdom and write a hundred books on wisdom, but unless you apply what you learned then its only words on a page. Life is not lived with intentions, but action."

~ Shannon L. Alder

(date)

"Good ideas stay with you until you eventually write the story."

~ Brian Keene

(date)

"The best fame is a writer's fame. It's enough to get a table at a good restaurant, but not enough to get you interrupted when you eat."

~ Fran Lebowitz

(date)

"Blessed are the weird people: poets, misfits, writers, mystics, painters, troubadours, for they teach us to see the world through different eyes."

~ Jacob Nordby

(date)

"Outlines are the last resource of bad fiction writers who wish to God they were writing masters' theses."

~ Stephen King

"I don't want to be a writer so I can write about my life. I want to be a writer to escape from it."

~ Candace Bushnell

"The good writing of any age has always been the product of someone's neurosis, and we'd have a mighty dull literature if all the writers that came along were a bunch of happy chuckleheads."

~ William Styron

(date)

"Writing, like life itself, is a voyage of discovery."

~ Henry Miller

(date)

"Writer's block? I've heard of this. This is when a writer cannot write, yes? Then that person isn't a writer anymore. I'm sorry, but the job is getting up in the fucking morning and writing for a living."

~ Warren Ellis

(date)

"Virtually every writer I know would rather be a musician."

~ Kurt Vonnegut Jr.

(date)

"Exercise the writing muscle every day, even if it is only a letter, notes, a title list, a character sketch, a journal entry. Writers are like dancers, like athletes. Without that exercise, the muscles seize up."

~ Jane Yolen

(date)

"The love between a writer and a reader is never celebrated."

~ Patricia Duncker

(date)

"The writer is either a practicing recluse or a delinquent, guilt-ridden one – or both. Usually both."

~ Susan Sontag

(date)

"I am a writer who came from a sheltered life. A sheltered life can be a daring life as well. For all serious daring starts from within."

~ Eudora Welty

(date)

"Writers don't need tricks or gimmicks. At the risk of appearing foolish, a writer sometimes needs to be able to stand and gape at this or that thing- a sunset or an old shoe- in absolute and simple amazement."

~ Raymond Carver

(date)

"The greatest part of a writer's time is spent in reading... to write."

~ Samuel Johnson

(date)

"No book can ever be finished. While working on it we learn just enough to find it immature the moment we turn away from it"

~ Karl R. Popper

(date)

"Writers end up writing about their obsessions. Things that haunt them; things they can't forget; stories they carry in their bodies waiting to be released."

~ Natalie Goldberg

(date)

"A writer never has a vacation. For a writer, life consists of either writing or thinking about writing."

~ Eugène Ionesco

(date)

"It took me a while to finish a book. Too long. And you know, it doesn't matter how good a writer you are unless you finish what you start! I think this is the hardest part for people who want to write."

~ Laini Taylor

(date)

"Life is painful and disappointing. It is useless, therefore, to write new realistic novels. We generally know where we stand in relation to reality and don't care to know any more."

~ Michel Houellebecq

(date)

"Being a writer is a good, good thing."

~ Shannon Hale

(date)

"I have yet to see a piece of writing, political or non-political, that does not have a slant. All writing slants the way a writer leans, and no man is born perpendicular."

~ E.B. White

(date)

"That thing you had to force yourself to do-the actual act of writing-turns out to be the best part."

~ Anne Lamott

(date)

"No writing is wasted: the words you can't put in your book can wash the floor, live in the soil, lurk around in the air. They will make the next words better."

~ Erin Bow

(date)

"You don't need to wait for inspiration to write. It's easier to be inspired while writing that while not writing..."

~ Josip Novakovich

(date)

"A person who publishes a book willfully appears before the populace with his pants down. If it is a good book nothing can hurt him. If it is a bad book nothing can help him."

~ Edna St. Vincent Millay

(date)

"All writers should be put in a box and thrown in the sea."

~ Gordon B. Hinckley

(date)

"I don't think writers are sacred, but words are. They deserve respect. If you get the right ones in the right order, you might nudge the world a little..."

~ Tom Stoppard

(date)

"If you won't write the classics of tomorrow, well, we will not have any."

~ Anne Rice

(date)

"For a writer, it seems a help rather than a hindrance to be at least a little crazy. Who but a crazy person would carve out a very private, quiet place in the world, only to pour his/her innermost thoughts and emotions onto a page for the entire world to examine? Even in fiction, we give a map to our most secret feelings. Why do writers do it? Perhaps because we'd be crazier still if we didn't."

~ Leland Dirks

THOUGHTS AND NOTES

(date)

January
February
March
April
May
June
July
August
September
October
November
December

"If someone loves your book, it increases the chance that he or she will look at mine. So there is no competition between writers. Another writer's success helps build a larger readership for all of us."

~ David Farland

(date)

"Write the book you have been trying to find but have not found."

~ Anne Rice

(date)

"I sometimes think it is because they are so bad at expressing themselves verbally that writers take to pen and paper in the first place"

~ Gore Vidal

(date)

"For any writer who wants to keep a journal, be alive to everything, not just to what you're feeling, but also to your pets, to flowers, to what you're reading."

~ May Sarton

(date)

"Writer's block results from too much head. Cut off your head. Pegasus, poetry, was born of Medusa when her head was cut off. You have to be reckless when writing. Be as crazy as your conscience allows."

~ Joseph Campbell

(date)

"A writer is a world trapped in a person."

~ Victor Hugo

(date)

"An original writer is not one who imitates nobody, but one whom nobody can imitate."

~ François-René de Chateaubriand

(date)

"Asking a working writer what he thinks about critics is like ask-ing a lamp-post what it feels about dogs."

~ John Osborne

(date)

"Who am I? I'm just a writer. I write things down. I walk through your dreams and invent the future. Sure, I sink the boat of love, but that comes later. And yes, I swallow glass, but that comes later."

~ Richard Siken

(date)

"I am a writer perhaps because I am not a talker."

~ Gwendolyn Brooks

(date)

"Play around. Dive into absurdity and write. Take chances. You will succeed if you are fearless of failure."

~ Natalie Goldberg

(date)

"Everything a writer learns about the art or craft of fiction takes just a little away from his need or desire to write at all."

~ Raymond Chandler

(date)

"The writer can grow as a person or he can shrink. ... His curiosity, his reaction to life must not diminish. The fatal thing is to shrink..."

~ Norman Mailer

(date)

"You become [a] writer by writing. It is a yoga."

~ R.K. Narayan

(date)

"All writers have this vague hope that the elves will come in the night and finish any stories."

~ Neil Gaiman

(date)

"Every good writer I know needs to go into some deep, quiet place to do work that is fully imagined."

~ Jonathan Franzen

(date)

"I've been writing about a subject I love as long as I can remember. I couldn't be happier knowing that young people are reading my books. More important to me is I've enjoyed so much writing them."

~ Walter Farley

(date)

"I'm not a very good writer, but I'm an excellent rewriter."

~ James A. Michener

(date)

"If you are a writer you locate yourself behind a wall of silence and no matter what you are doing, ...you can still be writing, because you have that space."

~ Joyce Carol Oates

(date)

"A writer who writes, knows peace, lives connected to truth."

~ Coco J. Ginger

(date)

"Writing isn't just a job that stops at six thirty... It's a mad, sexy, sad, scary, ruthless, joyful, and utterly, utterly personal thing. ...All of my life connects to the writing. All of it."

~ Russell T. Davies

(date)

"If you wish to be a writer, write."

~ Epictetus

(date)

"The young writer would be a fool to follow a theory. Teach yourself by your own mistakes; people learn only by error. The good artist believes that nobody is good enough to give him advice."

~ William Faulkner

(date)

"A writer doesn't solve problems. He allows them to emerge."

~ Friedrich Dürrenmatt

(date)

"Every reader finds himself. The writer's work is merely a kind of optical instrument that makes it possible for the reader to discern what, without this book, he would perhaps never have seen in himself."

~ Marcel Proust

(date)

"You are either born a writer or you are not."

~ Cormac McCarthy

(date)

"I have always been a huge admirer of my own work. I'm one of the funniest and most entertaining writers I know."

~ Mel Brooks

(date)

"But once an idea for a novel seizes a writer... it's like an inner fire that at first warms you ...but then begins to eat you alive, burn you up from within. ... The only way to put it out is to write the book."

~ Dean Koontz

(date)

"Writers write to influence their readers, their preachers, their auditors, but always, at bottom, to be more themselves."

~ Aldous Huxley

(date)

"Great writers, I discovered, were not to be bowed down before and worshipped, but embraced and befriended."

~ Stephen Fry

(date)

"A writer need not devour a whole sheep in order to know what mutton tastes like, but he must at least eat a chop. Unless he gets his facts right, his imagination will lead him into all kinds of nonsense, and the facts he is most likely to get right are the facts of his own experience."

~ W. Somerset Maugham

(date)

THOUGHTS AND NOTES

(date)

January	July
February	August
March	September
April	October
May	November
June	December

"Writing is a form of personal freedom. In the end, writers will write not to be outlaw heroes of underculture but mainly to save themselves..."

~ Don DeLillo

(date)

"Writer advice... Write. Finish things. Go for walks. Read a lot + outside your comfort zone. Stay interested. Daydream. Write."

— Neil Gaiman"

(date)

"Hardly anybody ever writes anything nice about introverts. Extroverts rule. This is rather odd when you realise that about nineteen writers out of twenty are introverts."

~ Ursula K. Le Guin

(date) ____________

"But this I know, the writer who possesses the creative gift owns something of which he is not always master."

~ Charlotte Bronte

(date) ____________

"My advice to writers just starting out? Don't use semi-colons! They are transvestite hermaphrodites, representing exactly nothing. All they do is suggest you might have gone to college."

~ Kurt Vonnegut Jr

(date)

"Everything you invent is true: you can be sure of that. Poetry is a subject as precise as geometry."

~ Julian Barnes

(date)

"Who here wants to be a writer?' I asked. Everyone in the room raised his hand. 'Why the hell aren't you home writing?' I said..."

~ Leon Uris

(date)

"Anyone who is going to be a writer knows enough at fifteen to write several novels."

~ May Sarton

(date)

"Writers do not have the privilege of sleep. There is always a story coming alive in their heads, constantly composing. Whether they choose it or not."

~ Coco J. Ginger

(date)

"The only reason for being a professional writer is you can't help it."

~ Leo Rosten

(date)

"When I was a little boy, they called me a liar, but now that I am grown up, they call me a writer."

~ Isaac Bashevis Singer

(date)

"To be a writer you have to write -- and no academic degree is going to do the writing for you. "

~ Michelle Richmond

(date)

"Tell your story. Don't try and tell the stories that other people can tell. Any starting writer starts out with other people's voices. But as quickly as you can start telling the stories that only you can tell..."

~ Neil Gaiman

(date)

"All glory comes from daring to begin."

~ Ruskin Bond

(date)

"There is a rule for fantasy writers: The more truth you mix in with a lie, the stronger it gets."

~ Diane Duane

(date)

"Practically everybody in New York has half a mind to write a book - and does"

~ Groucho Marx

(date)

"Life has no plot. It is by far more interesting than anything you can say about it..."

~ Erica Jong

(date)

"Truth for anyone is a very complex thing. For a writer, what you leave out says as much as those things you include. What lies beyond the margin of the text?"

~ Jeanette Winterson

(date)

"Think of this - that the writer wrote alone, and the reader read alone, and they were alone with each other."

~ A.S. Byatt

(date)

"The reason a writer writes a book is to forget a book and the reason a reader reads one is to remember it."

~ Thomas Wolfe

(date)

"Advice to young writers who want to get ahead without any annoying delays: don't write about Man, write about a man."

~ E.B. White

(date)

"The first thing that distinguishes a writer is that he is most alive when alone."

~ Martin Amis

(date)

"Writing is a solitary business. It takes over your life. In some sense, a writer has no life of his own. Even when he's there, he's not really there."

~ Paul Auster

(date)

"Anyone who says writing is easy isn't doing it right."

~ Amy Joy

(date)

"A scene should be selected by the writer for haunted-ness-of-mind interest. If you're not haunted by something involuntary, as by a dream, a vision, or a memory, you're not interested or even involved."

~ Jack Kerouac

(date)

"I don't give a damn if my work is commercial or not...I'm the writer. If what I write is good, then people will read it."

~ John Fante

(date)

"I demand the right to write any character in the world that I want to write. I demand the right to be them, I demand the right to think them and I demand the right to tell the truth as I see they are."

~ Quentin Tarantino

(date)

"I tell aspiring writers that you have to find what you MUST write."

~ Rick Riordan

(date)

"You do not have to love writing to write a book, but you must love your story. Choose the story you will share in your book and identify who will benefit from reading your story. Talk it or write it. Get it done."

~ CaZ

(date)

"Writing well means never having to say, "I guess you had to be there."

~ Jef Mallett

(date)

"As a writer, I like the list of "things to strive for" that Richard Yates kept above his typewriter:

genuine clarity
genuine feeling
the right word
the exact English sentence
the eloquent detail
the rigorous dramatization of story"

~ Richard Yates

THOUGHTS AND NOTES

(date)

(date)

January
February
March
April
May
June
July
August
September
October
November
December

"For your information, a good novel can change the world. Keep that in mind before you attempt to sit down at a typewriter. Never waste time on something you don't believe in yourself."

~ John Fante

(date)

"Never annoy an inspirational author or you will become the poison in her pen and the villian in every one of her books."

~ Shannon L. Alder

(date)

"It's not enough to write simply because you think it would be neat to be published. You have to be compelled to write. If you're not, nothing else that you do matters."

~ Rick Riordan

(date)

"It is necessary to write, if the days are not to slip emptily by. How else, indeed, to clap the net over the butterfly of the moment?"

~ Vita Sackville-West"

(date)

"My mind turned by anxiety, ...from its scrutiny of blank paper, is like a lost child–wandering the house, sitting on the bottom step to cry."

~ Virginia Woolf

(date)

"Don't waste time waiting for inspiration. Begin, and inspiration will find you."

~ H. Jackson Brown Jr.

"Writers are not just people who sit down and write. They hazard themselves. Every time you compose a book your composition of yourself is at stake."

~ E.L. Doctorow

(date)

"When you write about what you dream, you become a writer."

~ A. SalehZ

(date)

"Writers perform an extremely important role: they make others dream, those who are unable to dream for themselves. And everyone needs to dream. Could there be any more important job in life than that?"

~ Félix J. Palma

(date)

"For he does his work alone and if he is a good enough writer he must face eternity, or the lack of it, each day."

~ Ernest Hemingway

"Good writing is remembering detail. Most people want to forget. Don't forget things that were painful or embarrassing or silly. Turn them into a story that tells the truth."

~ Paula Danziger

(date)

"I sometimes think my head is so large because it is so full of dreams."

~ Joseph Merrick

(date)

"You can't really succeed with a novel anyway; they're too big. ...You can, however, write a perfect sentence now and then. I have."

~ Gore Vidal

(date)

"Often we write down a sentence too early, then another too late; what we have to do is write it down at the proper time, otherwise it's lost."

~ Thomas Bernhard

(date)

"The generalizing writer is like the passionate drunk, stumbling into your house mumbling: I know I'm not being clear, exactly, but don't you kind of feel what I'm feeling?"

~ George Saunders

(date)

"Never to write a line that's not your own..."

~ Edmond Rostand

(date)

"Writer's block is just a symptom of feeling like you have nothing to say, combined with the rather weird idea that you should feel the need to say something."

~ Hugh MacLeod

(date)

"Talent is extremely common. What is rare is the willingness to endure the life of the writer."

~ Kurt Vonnegut Jr

(date)

"A writer is a dangerous friend. ...We mean you no harm, but what you know and what you've done is unavoidably fascinating to us. ...Choose the stories you tell to your writer friends carefully."

~ Randy Murray

(date)

"I'm either going to be a writer or a bum."

~ Carl Sandburg

(date)

"Imagine a canvas for a lyrical, magical farce, for a pantomime, and translate it into a serious novel. Drown the whole thing in an abnormal, dreamy atmosphere, in the atmosphere of great days..."

~ Charles Baudelaire

(date)

"The artist must...make posterity believe that he never existed."

~ Gustave Flaubert

(date)

"One of the gifts of being a writer is that it... motivates you to look closely at life, at life as it lurches by and tramps around."

~ Anne Lamott

(date)

"Through the act of writing, a writer learns more about himself than he could ever imagine."

~ Rob Bignell

(date)

"Have you written anything I know? A dreadful question. Do you ask a surgeon if he has saved the life of anyone you know? Consider it is enough to be a writer and ask about the weather."

~ CaZ

(date)

"An unpublished writer should doubt themselves. And then, having doubted, they should take up their pen and ...make it better."

~ Johnny Rich

(date)

"Whatever our theme in writing, it is old and tried. Whatever our place, it has been visited by the stranger, it will never be new again. It is only the vision that can be new; but that is enough."

~ Eudora Welty

(date)

"I read obsessively when I'm writing. ...I need fixed stars to navigate by, otherwise I get lost in the blankness of the page."

~ Lev Grossman

(date)

"The blank page, otherwise known as the vast playground of the writer's imagination."

~ J.L. Bond

(date)

"You need to establish a degree of privacy and solitude in order to write."

~ Pamela Glass Kelly

(date)

"Writing is the dragon that lives underneath my floorboards. The one I incessantly feed for fear it may turn and devour my ass. Writing is the friend who doesn't return my phone calls; the itch I'm unable to scratch; a dinner invitation from a cannibal; elevator music for a narcoleptic. Writing is the hope of lifting all boats by pissing in the ocean. Writing isn't something that makes me happy like a good cup of coffee. It's just something I do because not writing, as I've found, is so much worse."

~Quentin R. Bufogle

THOUGHTS AND NOTES

(date)

(date)

January	July
February	August
March	September
April	October
May	November
June	December

"Fiction, like sculpture or painting, begins with a rough sketch. One gets down the characters and their behavior any way one can, knowing the sentences will have to be revised...."

~ John Gardner

(date)

"I write because I love it, not because I excel at it. But because I write, I shall slowly excel at it."

~ Richelle E. Goodrich

(date)

"...nearly everything seems a letdown after a writer has finished writing something."

~ John Irving

(date)

"In order for a writer to succeed, I suggest three things - read and write - and wait."

~ Countee Cullen

(date)

"That's what we storytellers do. We restore order with imagination. We instill hope again and again and again."

~ Kelly Marcel & Sue Smith

(date)

"Everything you do helps you to write if you're a writer. Adversity and success both contribute largely to making you what you are. If you don't experience either one of those, you're being deprived of something."

Shelby Foote

(date)

"I have an object, a task, let me say the word, a passion. The profession of writing is a violent and almost indestructible one."

~ George Sand

(date)

"Writing is a way of making the writer acceptable to the world—every cheap, dumb, nasty thought, every despicable desire, every noble sentiment, every expensive taste."

~ William H. Gass

(date)

"A short story is a different thing altogether – a short story is like a quick kiss in the dark from a stranger."

~ Stephen King

(date)

"...at best, in the very smallest scheme, writing can provide a moment of grace, both for her who writes and him who reads, in a dark world."

~ Cecile Pineda

(date)

"...a writer should not so much write as embroider on paper; the work should be painstaking, laborious."

~ Anton Chekhov

(date)

"A writer's primary goal is to make sense. The bookstore's is to make cents."

~ Mokokoma Mokhonoana

(date)

"The most humble toiler on Wall Street makes more in a month than ninety percent of writers make in a year. A beggar on the street, seeing a writer shuffling toward him, will dig deep into his rags to see if he can spare a dime...."

~ Peter Mayle

(date)

"If the writer doesn't sweat, the reader will."

~ Mark Twain

(date)

"I dream that one day I would be a published writer and people would read my books - if not, I would be living in the mountains in a small hut, near a pond where swans swim, writing a diary for myself."

~ Srinidhi.R

(date)

"Writers of fiction embellish reality almost without knowing it."

~ Aljean Harmetz

(date)

"The writer must know for whom he writes, why he writes, and if his writing says what he means for it to say."

~ Harper Lee

"No one can call themselves a writer until he or she has written at least fifty stories."

~ David Foster Wallace

"Writing is not always a writer's playtime. It's actually a work in progress. Few understand this and mistakenly believe we're wasting time. But it's never a waste of time when doing what you love."

~ David Lucero

(date)

"Writers write because they're writers."

~ Brian A. McBride

(date)

"You have to let writing eat your life and follow it where it takes you. You fit into it; it doesn't fit neatly into your life. It makes you wild."

~ Natalie Goldberg

(date)

"Writing like this is a little like milking a cow: the milk is so rich and delicious, and the cow is so glad you did it."

~ Anne Lamott

(date)

"Writing is, a contest of knowing, of seeing the dream, of getting there, and of achieving what you set out to do. The simplest way... is to say what you mean as clearly and precisely as you know how."

~ Harper Lee

(date)

"I read not for entertainment but to feel what the writer has felt while writing even though if it was fiction."

~ Pushpa Rana

(date)

"Dreamworlds can maintain themselves only as glimpses. Once the writer transports the reader across the threshold, nothing that was promised can be delivered."

~ M. John Harrison

(date)

"I am a writer and I want to write."

~ Jane Bowles

(date)

"A writer is like a tuning fork: We respond when we're struck by something. The thing is to pay attention, to be ready for radical empathy."

~ Roxana Robinson

(date)

"The secret to good writing is to use small words for big ideas, not to use big words for small ideas."

~ Oliver Markus

(date)

"For the length of time it takes to write a book, you need to believe that you're the only writer in existence; the only one who matters. You need to shut yourself away and allow the creativity to build up...."

~ Martin Cosgrove

(date)

"There are no lungs like the ones that breathe poetry."

~ D. Antoinette Foy

(date)

"If you want to write, if you want to create, you must be the most sublime fool that God ever turned out and sent rambling. You must write every single day of your life. You must read dreadful dumb books and glorious books, and let them wrestle in beautiful fights inside your head, vulgar one moment, brilliant the next. You must lurk in libraries and climb the stacks like ladders to sniff books like perfumes and wear books like hats upon your crazy heads.

I wish you a wrestling match with your Creative Muse that will last a lifetime. I wish craziness and foolishness and madness upon you. May you live with hysteria, and out of it make fine stories – science fiction or otherwise. Which finally means, may you be in love every day for the next 20,000 days. And out of that love, remake a world."

— Ray Bradbury

THOUGHTS AND NOTES

(date)

(date)

January July

February August

March September

April October

May November

June December

"The great spy novelist John Le Carré suggested this axiom: The cat sat on the mat is not the beginning of a story. The cat sat on the dog's mat, is."

~ James Scott Bell

(date)

"People don't remember lessons. They remember stories."

~ Kamand Kojourid

(date)

"Poetry is a way of coming to know the realness of things; fiction is a way of coming to know the world of relationships; nonfiction is a way of coming to know the world of the mind."

~ Kelly Cherry

(date)

"...no good writing flows from a polluted well - you can write about monsters, but you can't be one..."

~ John Geddes

(date)

"A writer writes knowing that nothing else will elicit the same kind of satisfaction and personal triumph as molding the written word into a reader's great experience."

~ Richelle E. Goodrich

(date)

"An author really ought to have nothing but flowers in the room where he works."

~ Gaston Leroux

"...it's as if she holds the sides of her chest apart, exposes her beating heart. And even though everything wants to heal, to close over and protect the heart, the writer must keep it bare, exposed."

~ Helen Humphreys

(date)

"Fiction must convince our bodies for it to have any chance of convincing our minds."

~ Bonnie Friedman

(date)

"If you're going to fall in love with anyone, fall in love with a writer. Allow yourself to become immortalised in words."

~ Jamie L. Harding

(date)

"I write because writing is power. Writing is creation. When you write, you are as a god, a deity wielding his pen like a Harry Potter staff."

~ Jonathan Culver

(date)

"A true writer should be able to write about any color. It's the story they tell that should affect people, not the race."

~ Dee Dee M. Scott

(date)

"Writers aren't exactly people. They're a whole lot of people, trying to be one person."

~ F. Scott Fitzgerald

(date)

"By sheer force of will and some clever word placement, I can ...invoke emotions and ideas at a whim. ...It does not take a man and a woman to create. It just takes a writer."

~ Jonathan Culver

(date)

"Everything is practice. Every word you write and action you take is a chance to get better."

~ Jeff Goins

(date)

"Don't say you're a writer if you're not writing. Even if you're writing, don't call yourself a writer. Say instead, 'I write.' It's the verb that's important, not the noun."

~ Patti Digh

(date)

"Each book is a new book. I've never written it before and I have to teach myself how to write it as I go along. The fact that I've written books in the past seems to play no part in it."

~ Paul Auster

(date)

"When I am working on a book or a story I write every morning as soon after first light as possible. There is no one to disturb you and it is cool or cold and you come to your work and warm as you write."

~ Ernest Hemingway

(date)

"A creative writer is one for whom writing is a problem."

~ Roland Barthes

(date)

"When a writer is able to experience the whole range of human emotions... it creates a whole inventory of feelings and musings from which they can choose and infuse into their words and characters."

~ David Perry

(date)

"Every book I've read appears in my writing."

~ Rob Bignell

(date)

"The most difficult part about writing a book, aside from starting it, is often overcoming your self-doubt and fears. What is gained after you become an author is more than what you expect or imagine it to be."

~ CaZ

(date)

"Writing is the light of imagination playing over shadow of thoughts."

~ Khaled Talib

(date)

"The truly great writer does not want to write: he wants the world to be a place in which he can live the life of imagination. The first quivering word he puts to paper is the word of the wounded angel: pain."

~ Henry Miller

(date)

"That's what I love most about writers--they're such lousy actors."

~ Vincent H. O'Neil

(date)

"Your reason for writing a book comes from the heart, from your passion to serve a purpose. There is no reason to wait for perfection. Do not plan to write a perfect book – you will never finish it."

~ CaZ

(date)

"... a writer concocts a different story for every reader."

~ Mike Bryan

(date)

"Writing is not as solitary as one might think. When it finally dawns on us one day that our task as writers is to share what we know of the human spirit, we suddenly discover that we were never truly alone."

~ Hal Zina Bennett

(date)

"Sometimes you just have to stop writing. Even before you begin."

~ Stanisław Jerzy Lec

(date)

"Writing isn't necessarily a gift it is a passion. ...What keeps you coming back is that Zen moment when you enlightened your own self with a few cleverly arranged words...."

~ Shannon L. Alder

(date)

"Turn beliefs into action to achieve dreams!"

~ CaZ

(date)

"We should write because it is human nature to write. Writing claims our world. It makes it directly and specifically our own. We should write because humans are spiritual beings and writing is a powerful form of prayer and meditation, connecting us both to our own insights and to a higher and deeper level of inner guidance.
We should write because writing brings clarity and passion to the act of living. Writing is sensual, experiential, grounding. We should write because writing is good for the soul. We should write because writing yields us a body of work, a felt path through the world we live in.
We should write, above all, because we are writers, whether we call ourselves that or not."

— Julia Cameron

THOUGHTS AND NOTES

CHAPTER THREE

What's Next?

Congratulations! You did it! You have successfully created and nurtured a daily writing habit that will (and perhaps already has) take you well on your way to achieving your writing dreams.

What's next? These steps are excellent choices:

- **Continue writing every day!** Reach out to me and I'll happily connect you with resources and tools that will entice you to continue writing.
- **Write your book**! It is almost certain you have an idea now and are ready to take the next step: to. join the *Book Writer Success Bootcamp* and get the knowledge, guidance, and skills to get your idea clarified and your manuscript written.

- **Publish your book!** Once the manuscript is completed, join the *Publish-it Now! Boot Camp* to quickly and easily become a published author.
- **Get a Writing Coach!** At any point, consulting with a coach is a great way to clarify what you want to accomplish with your writing. Accountability, industry knowledge, guidance, and wisdom are benefits you will receive from becoming an author with the *Writer Success Coach.*

What's next? The choice is yours, just as it was your choice to begin this book. Writing is a calling. You have answered the call and it does not end until you say so.

I wish you every success you dream of and beyond. Keep on writing.

About the Author

What's your purpose? Your passion? I am CaZ, the writer success coach and am passionate about the power of story.

Are you a reader who dreams of becoming a writer? Are you a writer who dreams of becoming an author? My answer to these questions was a resounding YES! and life changing. I was that bookworm and avid reader and published-author-wannabe.

What changed? I did. I left the safety of trading hours for dollars and I took up my career as a technical writer and diva just in time to be part of the revolutionary changes print on demand brought to publishing. Two of my books, Purpose Powered People and Purpose to Authority, share aspects of my journey and explain how you can find and follow your own story and passion to become a published author.

Today, I live at the beach on Pleasure Island in North Carolina. I swim and dance the Carolina Shag. I enjoy living my dream to be a successful author and I support other writers in finding their own success.

I coach readers to become writers and writers to become authors. What's your story? I truly would like to know.

Social Media and Connection Info

www.TheWriterSuccessCoach.com

www.ManifestPublishing.com

Look for me on Facebook, LinkedIn, and Twitter.

Training and Coaching for Writers

Book Writer Success Boot camp

(www.bookwritersuccess.com)

Publish-it Now! Boot Camp

LIST OF WRITERS QUOTED

THOUGHTS AND NOTES

THOUGHTS AND NOTES

THOUGHTS AND NOTES

THOUGHTS AND NOTES

THOUGHTS AND NOTES

THOUGHTS AND NOTES

THOUGHTS AND NOTES

THOUGHTS AND NOTES

THOUGHTS AND NOTES

www.ingramcontent.com/pod-product-compliance
Lightning Source LLC
Chambersburg PA
CBHW050112280326
41933CB00010B/1062